Garfield
in the mood
for food

JIM DAVIS

Ballantine Books • New York

A Ballantine Book
Published by The Ballantine Publishing Group

Copyright © 1998 by PAWS, Incorporated.

All rights reserved under International and Pan-American Copyright
Conventions. Published in the United States by The Ballantine Publishing
Group, a division of Random House, Inc., New York, and simultaneously in
Canada by Random House of Canada Limited, Toronto.

Ballantine and colophon are registered trademarks of Random House, Inc.

www.randomhouse.com/BB/

Library of Congress Catalog Card Number: 98-96714

ISBN: 0-345-91568-2

Manufactured in the United States of America

First Edition: December 1998

10 9 8 7 6 5 4 3 2 1

WHAT ?! WHERE ?!

HE DID IT AGAIN

9-1 © 1979 United Feature Syndicate, Inc.

JIM DAVIS

MORNIN'
GOOD MORNING, IRMA

THE COFFEE'S STRONG, HON. YOU'D BETTER GET IT BEFORE IT GETS YOU
IS IT HOT?

YUP
THIS ISN'T ONE OF YOUR BETTER DINERS

10-19 © 1979 United Feature Syndicate, Inc.

JIM DAVIS

CATS ARE ALWAYS UP TO SOMETHING...

SNEAKING AROUND THE HOUSE, CHASING RUBBER BALLS...

LEARNING TO USE THE CAN OPENER!

MY LIFE HAS NEW MEANING!

BRRRRR

JIM DAVIS 5-23

JIM DAVIS 6-15

WHAT A DISASTER! CHOCOLATE SYRUP AND NO ICE CREAM!

© 1990 United Feature Syndicate, Inc.

OKAY, SO IT'S NOT A DISASTER

JIM DAVIS 7-25

JIM DAVIS 8-25

CAT FOOD

GARFIELD

© 1990 United Feature Syndicate, Inc.

CAT FOOD

GARFIELD

EMPTY

DOES THIS MEAN YOU'RE NOT GOING TO FEED ME?

GARFIELD

GULP!

MY COMPLIMENTS TO THE CAN OPENER

QUITE A LITTLE RAINSTORM WE HAD LAST NIGHT, EH, BOYS?

GEE, I HOPE NONE OF THE FOOD GOT WET

SALTINE?

THIS LOOKS LIKE A GOOD PLACE TO MAKE CAMP

MUNCH MUNCH MUNCH MUNCH

© 1992 United Feature Syndicate, Inc.

I **TOLD** YOU NOT TO EAT YOUR ICE CREAM ALL IN ONE BITE

JIM DAVIS 11-30

© 1992 United Feature Syndicate, Inc.

I'M GETTING ORGANIZED

TO EAT

EATEN

© 1992 United Feature Syndicate, Inc.

JIM DAVIS 12-5

MONDAY CHECK

JIM DAVIS 1-18

SPLUT!

HA!

FOOLED YOU!

© 1993 United Feature Syndicate, Inc.

WOULD YOU MIND ROLLING AROUND IN THESE BREAD CRUMBS WHILE I PREHEAT THE OVEN?

WHAT?! WOULD YOU RATHER BE GRILLED? FRIED?...WHAT?!

JIM DAVIS 1-5-94

A LONE HAMBURGER

IT'S SEPARATED FROM THE HERD

YOU NEVER LOSE THOSE HUNTING INSTINCTS

JIM DAVIS 4-8

YEEEOOOOW!

© 1994 PAWS, INC./Distributed by Universal Press Syndicate

JiM DAViS 9-13

GREETINGS, LADIES AND GERMS! WELCOME TO...

TAPPITY TAPPITY TAPPITY

SPLOT!

© 1994 PAWS, INC./Distributed by Universal Press Syndicate

THE DINNER SHOW

JiM DAViS 11-2

BAD NEWS, GARFIELD. I FORGOT TO BUY CAT FOOD!

OH, NO!

WHATEVER WILL I DO?!

WHAT HAPPENED TO ALL THE ALUMINUM FOIL?

DISGUISED AS A LEFTOVER, GARFIELD?

SHHHH! YOU'LL SPOOK THE MEATLOAF!

ATTENTION! STEP AWAY FROM THE BURGER! STEP AWAY FROM THE BURGER!

WOOP WOOP WOOP WOOP

A BURGER ALARM!

AH-HA

JIM DAVIS 3-18

TLOK TLOK

SMACK SMACK

SMACK SMACK

JIM DAVIS 4-8

TLOK TLOK

SMACK SMACK

SMACK ACK

PSST! ODIE! WANT SOME MORE PEANUT BUTTER?

ONCE, CATS WERE FEARLESS HUNTERS...

INDEPENDENT, STRONG AND PROUD

BUT, TODAY...

COULD YOU GET THE PLASTIC OFF THIS SLICE OF CHEESE?

JIM DAVIS 9-27

TWO VISIBLE DOUGHNUTS FOR ME

AND TWO **IN**VISIBLE DOUGHNUTS FOR YOU

GIVE ME ONE OF THOSE

NOW, NOW. DON'T BE GREEDY

JIM DAVIS 8-4

CLICK

CLICK

AND HERE WE ARE AT THE WISCONSIN CHEESE FESTIVAL

DIET TIME

JIM DAVIS 11-7

CRUNCH CRUNCH CRUNCH CRUNCH CRUNCH CRUNCH CRUNCH CRUNCH

www.garfield.com

CRUNCH CRUNCH CRUNCH CRUNCH CRUNCH CRUNCH

OKAY! YOU CAN HAVE SOMETHING BESIDES CELERY FOR A SNACK!

IF YOU INSIST

JIM DAVIS 11-12